ON THE EDGE OF GRACE

Don Fisher

ACKNOWLEDGMENTS

I am deeply grateful to the following print and online journals that have accepted my work.

Bryant Literary Review - *You Could Die Laughing*

Clark Street Review - *In Defense of Punk Rock, Taking It Back,* and *To the Guy Who Flipped Me Off On Route 116*

Illya's Honey - *The Artist, Canada Geese Against A Blue October Sky* and *The Frozen Painter*

Jerseyworks - *A.A. Meetings*

Muse - *Buzz Aldrin is Alive and Well*

New Rag Rising - *Aberrant Thoughts*

Raven's Perch - *Brick Houses*

Riversedge - *Ballgame*

Silkworm - *Graveyard Party, For Sutherland Springs, Picking My Grandmother Up* and *Never Lead a Cow Downstairs*

Sunspinner - *The Creative Process*

The Peralta Press - *Written At The Laundromat*

The Adirondack Review - *The Wooden Bird*

Spank the Carp - *Mother and Son*

Aberrant Thoughts, was a runner-up in the Springfield, MA Library Poetry Contest

The Creative Process, was a runner-up in the Poet's Seat Poetry Contest in Greenfield, MA

Animal Heart and *You Could Die Laughing* were chosen as finalists in the Pat Schneider Contest sponsored by Peregrine magazine.

Dark Ink Magazine - *Dark Hours,* and *Hank Williams In My Kitchen* (pending publication).

Straw Dogs' website published *Outside* as part of their *Pandemic Project.*

California Quarterly - *When*

After Happy Hour Review - *Night Shift.*

Congruent Spaces - *At the Rainbow Cafe Teen Canteen in Chamberlain, South Dakota 1957.*

The Dance and *Lifeline* appeared on the Springfield, MA Library website as part of their Write-Up Springfield Spotlight.

For Kathy Dunn and Pat Schneider

and

anyone else I've ever sat in a room and wrote with.
You know who you are!

Published by Human Error Publishing
www.humanerrorpublishing.com
paul@humanerrorpublishing.com

Copyright © 2021
by
Human Error Publishing
&
Donald Fisher

ISBN#: 978-1-948521-09-3

Cover design
by
Paul Richmond
and
Donald Fisher

Photos
Tara Dasso

Editing
Ellen Eller
Bud Fisher

Table of Contents

The Creative Process

I can't draw a stick man
he mocks me
my not well-drawn man
wiggles non-existent hips
taunts me
but he's only made of sticks.

I point this out
he reminds me
I created him.
I'm his trickster god

"You made me this way,"
he wails
shaking his thin arms
weeping a puddle of tears
collecting at his feet.

To make him feel better
I give him a boxy car
not quite round wheels
bumping along a road.
My slashing pen
gives him birds above
a quarter of a yellow sun
peeking from one page corner
from a small house
smoke curls from a chimney.

Happy now
so easily pleased.
If he gets down again
I will destroy him and his world.
I like being a trickster god.
Controlling something
even only a simple stick man.

"I love your work," he says.

"I love you."
He dances a happy jig
across the page.
It doesn't matter that he's crudely drawn.
He's something.

Aberrant Thoughts

Driving home the other night
I thought
how easy it would be
to drive off the approaching bridge.

I reached it
crossed it
took the right turn for the shortcut home
aberrant thought forgotten quickly
one of a thousand random thoughts.

Like throwing a Molotov cocktail
through the front window of my workplace
kissing the eyes of a woman named Angela
or shrimp in a sauce of tomato and basil
an old Graham Parker song
pushing and shoving
like a crowded rock concert
each one louder and rowdier than the last.

The show is General Admission. The doors open
there's a mad rush to my brain.

One stoner grabs a great seat up close
"Dude," he says, "learn to play the guitar."
Another next to him, hisses
"Don't trust anyone."

The Artist

He throws pans across the room
slams plates
skids around the kitchen with a sharp knife
calls the wait staff "useless fucks."

His misogyny?
Don't even go there.

"But his sauces rock!"
say the folks at the front tables
"his scampi is to die for."
Fine, I reply
you work with him.

Written At The Laundromat

At the laundromat
seven pairs of eyes
stare back
black cordoroys
brought to the front
replace the white t-shirt
pass behind
the glass cornea
as close to a wink as I'll get.

Infidelity

If my mind stopped it would leave skid marks
I want it to shut down like a furnace
then I would sleep for a week.
I would spoon with my loneliness
make love to it when I woke up.

The noise of the two of us fucking
would wake the neighbors.
Then self pity gets jealous and slits my pillows,
pride leaves threatening messages for me
(on one of them she calls me a bastard)

I'm having drinks with lust
meeting inertia within the hour.
It's all going to catch up with me soon.

Animal Heart

My heart's a tiger
pacing its' cage in
slow circles.

It rages
I weep in the morning
I don't understand
why it won't
let my mind crack the whip
to make it stand on its hind legs
or do stupid tricks
for a gaping crowd.
My heart does tricks for nobody.
It will not stand on its head
sing "I Put A Spell On You"
guzzling a glass of water.

I shouldn't weep.
Proud of my stubborn heart's refusal to dance
I should go where it leads me.

Canada Geese Against A Blue October Sky

I want to tell you about the V.

It is perfect
an arrow well-aimed by someone
towards somewhere.

You and I move forward in a like manner
directed by no one.
Towards we don't know where.
It's the journey?
Isn't it?
Isn't that the important part?
Do the geese cease their honking
to think about where they're headed?
Not that I know
nor do they stop to lament
that their necks are
too long
too green
too sleek.
Or that their honks are too nasal
not guttural enough.
Or to apologize for bumping
into each other in mid-air.
No goose guilt.

Their motto could well be
"it's all good."
Even the ragged, undulating V
works for them.
They still get where they want to go.
"It's all good," they cry out, "it's all good."

Why I Never Write When I Shouldn't

I am happy tonight
really
I swear.
I am also tired
creatively barren
gassy.

All leads up
to I can't
won't
shouldn't write.
Maybe the last of these
because of what might happen.

The last time I wrote when I shouldn't
it all got away from me
the townsfolk went after it
with torches, pitchforks.

This was after a rabble rousing meeting
in the town square
replete with shouting
waving
rabble rousing.

A ballot question
showed up last November.
Should I be allowed to write
when I shouldn't be writing?
Those understanding the question
voted a resounding no.

The people have spoken.

Taking It Back

Her words strangled the air.
"You're a terrible writer,
shallow, stupid,
you have nothing important to say."
I took back the whole evening
broke apart
got up
threw on my clothes.
Sitting at the kitchen table
I choked up the delicious dinner she'd made.
Ass end out the kitchen door
her back to me as she cooked.

I took back every nice thing I'd said to her
stuffed them inside
to save them for someone else.

The love poems I wrote her
are trees again.

I took back the evening
the whole summer.
We even got out of the shower,
reapplied sticky bug spray
returned to the fireworks
where purple
red flowers
closed up to a stem in the sky
then shrank back to earth.

Ballgame

Up on a ridge
overlooking the town
I heard
before I saw
the batter, batter
swing, swing, patter
of a little league ball game.
I looked down
on a gray diamond
stitched on a blanket of green.

Intrigued
I drove down
I arrived in the middle
of this amazing rally
crack   crack   crack
balls hit
high enough
over heads of infielders
who tried gamely
extending their arms
leaping
on the edge of grace.

Until the umpire
the only adult on the field
called the game
on account of darkness.

A.A. Meetings

I envy them,
coming out of church basements
milling around outside
chain-smoking
talking
uncertain
with nowhere else to go.

They linger in groups of three or four,
semi circles,
old habits dying hard.
Now there is no bottle of red wine
passing around
no Thunderbird
or Bud kingers.

They talk too loud
go out for coffee
close the place.

I envy their experience
their secrets
carried deep
inside their massive guts
and chainsaw coughs.

The only meeting I attended
a middle-aged guy
danced to *Feeling Like Breaking Up Somebody's Home*
in long, leaping circles.

Graveyard Party

I wonder why teenagers
like to party in graveyards
old tombstones jut out
stained broken teeth.

Is it the delicate chink
of beer bottle on marble?
the quiet spit of a match?
Or is it because it's the only place they know
where no one will bother them?
The dead do not click their tongues
or roll their eyes disapprovingly.
Who else knows more
about life's brevity?
One rotting thumb raised in salute
to an opened beer
or lit joint.
When one young woman down on her knees
with shaking hands fishes out
her boyfriend's pale white cock,
the dead do not judge.

In the dark, these kids
can't see each other.
One tries out the word "motherfucker"
again and again,
it feels good.
Thick night air traps the curse
holds it
throws it back.

He catches it neatly
tosses it hand to hand
a too hot stone
drops it in the grass
it rolls end over end
stops
glows red for a moment

then dies forever.
They all laugh.

The young woman returns with her boyfriend
her head down
jacket clutched around herself
"I'm a priest," she jokes
"I was hearing his confession,"
smiling as hoarse laughter
rebounds to her.

There it is.
Laughter sounds better
at night
in a graveyard.

Community Shower

At summer camp
Terry laughed at everyone's penis.

Bob's
short knob like
squat
like Bob himself.

Terry made a big deal
laughed and pointed.

1969
back then
mine
was shy withdrawn
noticed
in attempts to not be noticed.

Brick Houses

I love brick houses
you can see
how they were built.

Imagine
guys in stained white overalls
troweling
laying each brick in place.

Other houses
reveal nothing.
Some people would
could
tell me how they were put up.
They'd be right.

They should write their own poems
about mixing cement
laying foundation
putting up drywall.

Me?
I'll write what I know
of brick houses.

To The Guy Who Flipped Me Off
On Route 116

I know, I know
I responded badly.
Tired, unwell, driving home
skies gray.

I wore a half-smile. I quickly extended
right arm, middle finger
to your level.

Maybe you laughed as you walked away
maybe I did
both feeling better
venting
without doing each other serious harm.
Of course I thought to myself
"whoa that was weird"
not much beyond that, at least not then.

Four days later I still see your face
eyes hard with rage
words thoughts buzzing behind
bushy gray beard
my rear-view mirror showed
you walking away down the middle of the road
khaki green backpack hiked over shoulders.

I hope your next day was better
Mine was. The sun came out
for a while
I hope you fell asleep in the grass
dreaming of a woman you once knew
the light rain that woke you
could have easily been her kiss.

Never Lead A Cow Downstairs

Little known factoid: You can lead a cow upstairs but you cannot lead it downstairs.

When I was young my father tried to lead a cow downstairs to keep it out of the rain.

The animal broke its front legs, milk ran out of its nose.

Later that night, drunk at dinner Dad warned. "Never lead a cow downstairs, they will never forgive you."

In Dad's later years I saw he was right. The cow's eyes, once soft and friendly, became hard, accusing.

"I once enjoyed the feel of your hands on my side," the eyes said. "I loved the way they caressed me when you stole my milk. Now I see only hands leading me down stairs."

Mother And Son

His twin brother
died at birth.
His mother says "Your dead brother
is so handsome
successful.
Why can't you be more like him?"

"Handsome," the son shrieks,
"He never got the chance to be handsome!"
"I know he was," is the response,
"I know when they tore him out of my body
he was handsome.
A mother just knows these things."

"He's dead," he shouts.
The mother shouts back
"And very good at it.
There's great integrity
in knowing what you are good at
and sticking to it.
Look at his beautiful tombstone."

The Wooden Bird

A wooden bird hatched from a wooden egg. The mother looked at it, thought, "If it fell to the ground and splintered, the pieces would make an excellent nest."

Don't judge her. She was not expecting what she got. She was thinking of making a home for a child that would never fly, made of oak, hard-heavy like a door. Not balsa which, if a breeze rose, would be light enough to stay elevated. It moved slower than other birds. When the rains arrived, what then?

For all these reasons the mother bird nudged her wooden offspring from the nest, using the splinters to build a lovely new home that other mother birds envied. "It was made from my wooden child," she would sing. "I loved him. He was beautiful, but wooden. What else could I do?"

Rhetoric

1943
Van Sickle Junior High
Springfield, Massachusetts.
On Wednesday nights they show newsreels
before a featured movie.

My father and his cousin
Bobby are there one night.
They are still kids.

During a newsreel account
of the Allied forces in Europe
Bobby
caught up in the moment
jumps out of his chair
taken over by patriotic fervor
shouts, "Give it to 'em boys!"

It could have been any of us.

During the Spanish Civil War
American lefties
jumped out of their chairs
instant converts to the good fight.
But it was a war
like any other
and people died fighting it.

None of us is above getting swept up
like Bobby in that basement
all those years ago.

We want things to be simple.
We want to be on the side of good.
Like it's a choice we can make
salting food or not
the tan slacks or the dark gray.
I even want this poem to be simple.

30

For Sutherland Springs

This poem is not about angels
or about devils
it is only about us
our own limitless capacity
for good and evil.

This poem is not a prayer
it will not change the world
or anyone's mind.

This poem is shot from a gun
but it doesn't take a life.

This poem sits
on both sides of the fence.

This poem is reasonable
even-minded
it sees both sides of an issue.
This poem is fed up
it is a rant
a diatribe.

This poem is a spitball
launched at God
it is a drop
in an endlessly deep bucket.
pock   pock   pock.

This poem walks into a church
hands out milk and cookies
for everyone.

This poem walks into a church
and takes a seat
like every week.

This poem walks into a church.

This poem walks into a wall.

This poem walks away.
Everyone walks away.

In Praise Of Punk Rock

Sometimes I wish anger came more easily
reachable
a book on a shelf
consequences be damned.

Many friends have anger issues.
I ran into one
for the first time in over a year.
He behaved like an absolute dick.
My anger
would have been entirely appropriate.
When he left I could not stop laughing
Sun comes up
moon comes out
my old friend is an ass.
It was almost comforting
in an "all is right with the world" kind of way.

My worst nightmares are rages
directed at someone else
or theirs at me.
I wake up shaking
in a minute or two
I realize it was a dream.

This leads to my love of punk rock.
The angrier the better.
Get pissed off for me.
If anger came easily
I would not need the Clash
X-Ray Spex
Flipper
The Slits
Bad Brains
L7
DOA.
Thanks.
Each time I put in a CD

I know with every amphetamine guitar riff
breakneck tempo
hoarse shout
you're doing it for me.
I raise a glass to you
but I will not throw it against the wall.
Instead, I step to the sink
rinse it out thoroughly
put it in the dishwasher.

Buzz Aldrin Is Alive And Well

It all comes down to sky.
Foreboding gray
clear blue
smeared thumbprint of cloud
empty closet
to hang whatever metaphor you wish.

The first to notice sky,
were they terrified?
Were most ordinary
stars omens?
Did these first ponder their smallness before
all else?
Or did they shrug
continue hunting
or screwing or whatever
to pass the time.
Face it, metaphysics takes a back seat
to hunger or lust.

But eventually
someone unfed
unfucked
did think about it enough
to want to know more.
Some were rewarded for their efforts
with a good, old-fashioned public execution.
The last words they likely heard were:
"The world is flat, you heretic.
How could we stay on it if it weren't."
The seekers were not given time
to come up with the word gravity.
Besides, the response would have likely been
"gravi-what?"

I look up, see sky
think, "cool."
I appreciate clouds

see shapes and forms.
I wonder what color blue
would a sky like today's be?
Cerulean?
I don't know.

By the time pictures
proved the shape of the planet
we already knew.
We stared at the stark black, white photos:
"Yup round, like they said,"
and off we went to bed.

But some had flying dreams.
Glorious where we were high and safe
then came to running stops along the ground.
We rode satellites
shook hands with stars.
My brother, my sister and I were all awakened
plopped down on the sofa
to watch Neil Armstrong take that one small step.
I remember little.

Neil Armstrong returned famous
Buzz Aldrin came back awed.
He drank too much
had a nervous breakdown.
Think about it: what
on this planet
could match what he saw up there?
Was he disappointed in everything?

He came around though
and one day saw earth and sky
with equal wonder.

Ode To Sam Peckinpah

Is it possible to create great art without being a dick?

Hemingway
Picasso
Jim Morrison
Miles Davis
all dicks.

You would not want to
sit next to them on a bus.
Peckinpah
would adjust his dirty headband
chug bourbon
snort lines of coke
tell you to fuck off.

I don't have many anecdotes
about those other guys.
But Peckinpah, he could be
a complete bastard.

On the set of *The Wild Bunch*
he bullied
intimidated.

It's about outlaws
looking to get rich.
By the end
you've spent a lifetime with them
you want them to live
as you watch every bullet
tear into their leathery hides.

Or this story from the set:
when reaching the scene on the bridge
a crew member complained
"Christ, you're not going to blow up another bridge!"
"It's not just another bridge," was his response.

"It's the way you blow it up."
Suspended for an eternity
men and horses
dropping in slow motion
was the way he blew it up.

To get beauty
maybe he needed to be
a little bit of an asshole.
Maybe the same thing is true
for *A Farewell to Arms*
Guernica
Kind of Blue.
Maybe that's what got Peckinpah
from point A to point B.

His movies got weirder
he never matched *Wild Bunch*.
Hard living caught up with him.

It was probably the only way he knew.
You and I know other ways,
does that make us
better?
smarter?
luckier?

The old bastard
if I ever met him
I'd hate his guts.
But not
before telling him
how that scene
at the end of
Ride The High Country
with Joel McRea
dying
dropping
to the bottom
of the screen

38

huge blue mountains
behind him
still gives me shivers.

You Could Die Laughing
for Sarah Purnell and especially for Anne

I told a co-worker about a mutual friend dying.
She thumbed away a tear.
"Death is stupid," she said.

Death is stupid
like stubbing your toe in a dark room
when there's a light switch right beside you.
Or driving the wrong way down a one-way street.

The end of anything is stupid.
The only mutual relationship I ever had,
the end was heartbreaking.
It was also stupid.
I mean why?
Why end it?
My inner brat rushed out and stamped his foot.
"Stay with me or I'll hold my breath until I die.
I don't want anyone else, I want you.
This is stupid."

Death is the ultimate stupidity.
The exploding cigar at the end of a long smoke.
A years-long daisy eventually squirts water in your eye.
A banana peel you miss because it's around a corner.
Death is stupid.

Signal right and make a left.
Look one way not the other.
A stupid way to go.
If you believe in heaven
you go and there's a special room.
You get a seat next to the guy
who plugged in his radio above the bathtub.
Stupid, right?

My mother losing her memory is stupid.
Getting old is stupid.

Maybe this poem is stupid
and years from now
will stupid people scratch their heads over it?

It's okay
we're all stupid sometimes.
On occasion it feels like life
is nothing more than a struggle to outrun
our dumbness.
To transcend our stupid selves.
I mean everyday stupid
not monumental stupid
not evil stupid.

It's okay if you buy sun-dried peppers
instead of sun-dried tomatoes,
bubble bath instead of body wash.
It won't be the last stupid thing.
Chances are the very last thing
will be
mind-numbingly
irrevocably
stupid.
You could die laughing.

A Bit Of Conversation Overheard While Standing On A Corner Outside The Frozen Yogurt Stand In A Nearby Trendy Town

"...well, I spent a summer in London one year
    for three weeks..."

I finger the hole in the toe of my right sneaker
think about how everyone
in this town has spent a summer in London
    one year for three weeks.

Here

I don't write tonight
instead
I sit and smile.

The heat presses down
my shorts are torn
my sandals worn.

This is tangible
like my feeling for you
corporeal.

I play with it
shape it
let it sit by me
a comforting hand
on my shoulder
a head resting
against my chest
listening to my heart
it's there all right
trust me.

I stroke your black curtain of hair
you lay there for a while.

Living With Winter

I learn to live with winter
driving on snowy mornings
I put more English on my turns
tap the brake
when getting ready to stop.

I laugh when my car shimmies
back and forth
a ball of paper at a white cat's mercy.

On cold nights before a heavy snowfall
I go outside and wait
for that first not-alike snowflake
I don't care if it takes all night.

In the hallway
my boots kicked off
my hat, coat
tossed off
but still giving off
cold weather smell.
I'll make tea.

If I plan like this
I'll get around to doing it
living in the poem
surrounded by its words
tall black trees with only a few branches.

Musings On Love And Music

Thinking about records
about vinyl
how I miss it
it had texture
heft.

Back then
after buying
I would carry albums home
on the bus
proudly displaying
musical tastes
to anyone who cared.
No one did.

Once home
I would hold them
run my thumbnail
along the edge
split the plastic wrap.
A smell
faint
but it was there.
My heart would swell with anticipation.

I would pull the record
from its sleeve.
Black grooves
deep enough
to hold secrets.

With two hands
I would put it on the spindle
watch the needle swing silently
hover
slowly lower
like a lover.

I would listen.

Twenty minutes later
second side
I would listen again.

One snowy night
home from a workplace
holiday party
high on coke
I lay down with my headphones
listened to the Replacements
Let It Be.
I have never loved
an album more than that one.
It was a good night
in my twenties
I could live that way
be okay the next day.

Those days
along with vinyl
are gone.

Loving music meant
reluctantly switching
from vinyl
to cassettes
to CDs.

Is it an exaggeration
saying that my breakup with vinyl
was the start of adulthood?

It happened
around the time I met Cindy.

I loved her
I needed her like air
but I was

air conditioning
comfortable
needed sometimes
eventually not
I could never talk about music with her.
Vinyl was getting scarce
so I bought cassettes.

I loved Jen
angry at the world Jen
not righteous Clash angry-
not always,
she raged
but never at me
not once.
When she told me
she didn't love me back
it was gently
with compassion.
She recorded a cassette
P.J. Harvey on one side
Lisa Germano on the other.
"Some Damn Strong Women"
she wrote on the label
gave it to me.
This was not a small thing.

Grace and I had music
not much else.
Swore she loved me
but I was never going to love her back
a thousand songs
I could have used to tell her
instead I was silent
not nearly as brave
as songs.

Long distance Allie
my heart swelled again.
I would call

recite poetry.
I loved her
she loved me back.

Good start
but not enough.
A hundred songs
say the same thing.
Cavemen drew pictures
on cave walls
telling the same story
expectations
disappointment
stumbling into the rain
outside
raging
weeping
singing.

Risotto

When making a risotto the Arborio rice should, by the time the meal is cooked, have a creamy texture; almost pourable. The rice should have some bite to it still. Make sure your broth is hot, and the rice mixture is simmering. Stay close to the stove, don't abandon the rice for too long or else it will stick to the pan. You should stir it constantly, but I do find myself stepping away for half a minute. All in all, the process should take about twenty minutes. In the last ten of these you can add whatever vegetables you like. Risottos are as versatile as pasta so use your imagination.

Risotto requires patience. You won't get it right the first time, but that shouldn't discourage you. It's not difficult. Why is it that I can slow my heart and my whirring thoughts and take the time to make risotto? Center myself in the kitchen. It is because I love it. And it is only an hour and a half of my life.

And then there is watching the mixture turn from one thing to another. The texture at the time the meal is finished doesn't last. What I don't eat becomes thicker and turns into something with a much gluier texture as it sits in the pan. It's never as good the second time around. It's as fleeting a pleasure as hearing *Wild Thing* on the car radio. Forgetting the song five minutes later, but remembering the feeling it gave you forever.

Life Work

I had a girlfriend
once
who insisted she was never going to die.

She would just keep going till she got it right
correcting
altering
shading
rearranging.

With hammer and nail she worked,
cleaned up
with broom and dustpan.

I was not the mess
I was the coat of paint that she decided didn't look right.
I got whitewashed over.

Look,
I was working as well.
It's not like my life didn't need it.

She was the contractor for that job
that used substandard materials
I had to let her go.
Since then I've spoken to her

once
in the middle of the conversation she interrupted herself
to berate the construction crew for the piss poor job
they were doing with her life work.

But you get what you pay for.

Lifeline

Raw cold
shoulders hunched
head down
stinging pellets of rain
here I am
hands stuffed into pockets
still here.

Waiting for the walk signal
clearing my throat
rinsing lettuce in a huge sink
shaking handfuls of it dry.

I walk everywhere
even treat myself
to one of those eclairs
at the food co-op.

One step in front of the other
my feet hurt
from standing so much
but heart and brain are happy
my feet forget they're tired
pull me forward
like a string
tugging me to the end of my life.

Alzheimers

My mother is
shrinking
folding
into herself.
Everything
about her is
smaller
including her voice.

These days
I can barely hear her.
Soon she will be mute.

Her legs will not touch the floor.
I will be able to hold her
in the palm of my hand.
They will lose her
at the home
and be very careful
about where they step.
They will take extra precautions
by keeping her in a shoe box
at the nurses station.
My shrinking mother.

There is a box
in our garage at home.
It is labeled funeral dress.
Inside is the dress we will bury my mother in.

In our garage
there is also a snow blower
a lawn mower
a weed whacker
seven or eight boxes of my stuff
a large rug on the floor
a mostly empty 25 lb. bag of bird seed.

Our second refrigerator
is plugged into the back wall.
There is pork tenderloin in its freezer
along with rolls for sandwiches
two tenderloin steaks.
In the refrigerator
butternut squash
a sweet potato
brussel sprouts
milk
eggs
kale
suet cakes
for the birds.

On top of the refrigerator is the box
that holds my mother's funeral dress.

A Sleuth Of Bears

He was a sleuth of bears. He only investigated bears and their habits. Why they did what they did. Until he decided to learn more about Ursa in the night sky and he was never seen again.

Some suggested that it was a conspiracy of lemurs that took him away. But a parliament of owls shook their heads and said, "no, lemurs do not plan beyond their next meal." Then a scourge of mosquitos interrupted, descending on all of them like a cloud. They all buzzed, "the sleuth of bears had sweet blood but we had nothing to do with his disappearance." The ferrets wanted to put their two cents in but all they talked of was the business of ferrets, nothing to do with the missing sleuth of bears. A maelstrom of salamanders darted in among the leaves and grass. "We miss the sleuth of bears," they insisted, "he was kind to us and was careful not to step on us." A walk of snails tried to be there but did not arrive in time. "It is our lot," they cried, "always late, always late." The sleuth of bears thought about all of them from time to time but the universe was staggeringly large and mind boggling and he decided to become a sleuth of stars instead.

Bill

We talk about getting older
it doesn't show on him.
He's a good six inches taller
blonde curls reaching
shoulders,
long broad good guy face
a tired, happy horse.

Large freckled hands
when we meet and depart
I take one of them
in both of mine.

He radiates towering, quiet strength.
Next to him I feel short,
doughy,
pliable.
I stay close,
hope some of him
rubs off.

Years ago
that yellow truck he drove,
he was drunk
yelling my name
burning rubber.
Everyone asks. "Who's that?"
I pretend I don't know
but I want to be in that truck,
leaning into the too quick turns,
screeching tires
let me drive.

Cliché

It will all come together someday
because you can't have one without the other
so I will write in clichés from now on
and that way everyone will know what I am talking about.
I will talk about the horse that you can lead to water
but the damn saddle is on the wrong damn horse
and the barn is locked after he is gone
and did you grow up in a barn
the one that you couldn't hit the broad side of
and then there was the horse of a different color
and one man's meat that turns out poisoning the other man
the one who is not an island
and people who need people
are they the same people who have excuses
that are like assholes because everyone has one
but you can't cheat an honest man
and there is one born every minute
and you can't live with 'em or without 'em
and every dog has his day
and a smile is just a frown turned upside down
and a stranger is just a friend you haven't met
and then there are the flies you caught using honey instead of vin-
egar
while you get handed a lemon and you make lemonade
then you get handed a life like a bowl of cherries
while outside there is a bird in the hand that is worth two in the
bush
in the yard where the grass is always greener on the other side
of the mountain that was made out of a molehill
but still good things come in small packages
those packages come in the mail that must go through wind and
rain and sleet and hail
and outside your cat ate the canary
in the coalmine
on the dog days of summer
when it was hot enough to fry an egg on the sidewalk
and that egg was laid because someone did not count their chickens
before they were hatched

but you have to break a few eggs to make an omelet
and nobody wants to know how the sausage is made
well it's made by strange bedfellows
who always depend on the kindness of strangers
who if they don't have anything nice to say say nothing at all
but we will cross the bridge when we get to it
and the chicken crossed the road to get to the other side
but that story goes in one ear and out the other
and up, and up, and away into the sky
that's red at night
so that all the sailors take delight
compared to a red sky at morning when they take warning
but they never went broke underestimating the intelligence
of the wagging tongue that bites itself
you can't have one without the other
and one thing leads to another
of good things that come in threes
but then you lose an eye for an eye a tooth for a tooth
and the pen is mightier than the sword
but even still beware of Greeks bearing gifts
because the only things for certain are death and taxes
but all roads lead to follow the leader
follow your heart
is a lonely hunter.

One Night

I could tell she was a townie, most everyone in the bar was. When the band played *Caledonia* she asked me to dance. I'd seen her earlier, while Dan and I played pool. She'd been playing the table next to ours. She had on a t-shirt that read "I've been to hell." We danced in a relaxed, loose way, stopping and starting with the chorus, "what makes your big head so hard". As the song ended she gave me a short clipped bow, it surprised me. It had dignity and grace; my return bow was abrupt. And then she went back to her table and I went back to mine.

Good Sheep

You see people doing their best to get by
call them sheep.

Let me swallow this last mouthful
of rich green grass
while I stand in this lovely meadow
and say you're sheep as well.

In your own way
you like the taste of grass.

We are sheep
dealing with the world as it is
not as we'd like it to be.

We don't want
to carry the horns of a steer.
We don't want
to be ridden like horses.
We don't want
to roll in filth like pigs.
We are sheep.

I am one.
I dream of mastering the bleat
making it lovely
more dulcet.

Others dream of becoming great sweaters
stand still and patient
for the shearing
a little offended when the wool is dyed.

We take care of our lambs
and of the other sheep
make sure they are safe
well fed.
Sometimes this is the best that we can do.

The border collie guards us
the good ones
let us choose where we graze.

If the collie
is a wolf
we can say so
point it out to anyone who will listen.

Or we can shit where he sleeps.

We have avenues open to us.
We do get angry
stomp our hooves
sound our lunatic bleat.

Feathers

I chase my thoughts
like a farmer chases chickens.

No luck.

I am left
with handfuls of brown and white feathers
nonetheless they look beautiful
when I drop them
onto mud and shit beneath me.

The Dance

I'm still learning
I tread on a few toes.
apologize too much.
The complicated stuff
where two people
swing each other around...
well, I once knocked someone senseless.

Now I know I can do it
for a time
slowly
I learned that last year.
My partner was patient
while I taught myself to be.
Our halting steps
were graceful
an assured tango.

The music was our lives
two very different songs
still being written
that was okay for a while
we danced until it wasn't
then stopped.

I Loved 'Ya

Yeah
well
I loved 'ya.

It was tormented
sad
quick
great.

We agreed
our first mutual
affair we'd had—
both of us in our early to mid-forties—
I didn't know whether
to be depressed
or happy about this fact.
I went with both
a lot.

I did love you
oh lord
did I ever.
And you responded
made me feel loved.
Even when we split
I felt loved.
Which was wonderful
heartbreaking at the same time.

Lovely confusion
confusing love
I said to friends
that I
wished that you cheated on me
so I could feel something
clear and pure
none of this muddied stuff.
But no
mud is there

it's water
soil
other people
everyday conversation
nothing simple

except what I felt at its purest
laughing after we made love
at how simple
it actually was
relief.

So I won't go to my grave
saying I was never loved
because there was you

the risotto with carrots and parsley
that I made
the crabcakes with roasted red pepper sauce
that you made.
We sat across the table from each other
while we ate
and music played in the background
maybe Bessie Smith
I can't remember what was playing.

I loved 'ya
'ya loved me back
we will probably
never see each other again
you're in Munich
I'm not.

Physical distance between us
that's our thing
even when we were lovers
maybe that's why it worked
for a while
and why it didn't
after a while.

Never Let Someone You Love
Read Your Tarot

In the restaurant she sat across from me and told me about
the Greek myths associated with the cards. I couldn't help
but apply each story to the two of us. Then she got sick and
I took her home. I laid in bed, stroked her hair but what
should have been transcendent was weird and awkward.
Within a week we agreed to keep our distance. Actually
managed to hold that promise the length of a summer. But
in September we met again and I tasted rainwater on her
lips under every covered doorway we came to. In the end we
said to hell with it splashed like kids, laughing. It felt good to
laugh, be with her and laugh.

Ode To My Left Hand

In the soup
of genes
blood
skin
muscle
a right-hander was made.

In the womb
I heard my mother's
muffled heartbeat
reached out with
my right hand—
even then.

On the day of her funeral
I stroked her cheek
with my right hand.
When I lie dying
my right hand
will control the morphine drip
while my left
lies quietly by my side.

But I will thank you, left hand
remind you that
when I pleasured myself
I always started with you.

When I ate a meal
you graciously gave the knife over
to the right
while he conceded the fork to you.
It was a pact.

You made gestures of kindness
told jokes that needed more than words
you never threw a slap

or a punch
only an occasional middle finger.

You held the backs of lovers' heads
while your nastier partner
wandered lower
wandered down
explored.

WHEN...

it rained outside.
When the sound of it
came through open windows.

When you lay
naked on the bed.
When I knelt on the bed
by your feet.

When I started
licking
kissing
your toes
worked
my way up
your arches
heels
calves
knees
the hollow
at the back of each knee.

There
you moaned
moved
like an ocean
in a storm.

The Forecast

"It's like the weather"
a friend says.
I tell her that some rainy mornings
it does make sense to stay in bed.
"Yes," she replies, "but forever?"

No
there are even mornings
when I'm reassured
by the tick tock
of rain on my car roof.
The snowfall
feels as much like a gift
as the first warm day of spring.

We were talking about relationships
and how to remember
that they're supposed to be fun.

I would wear a raincoat for you
tuck an umbrella under my arm
snap it open
when the time is right.
I'd wear layers of clothes
heavy boots
gloves and a woolen hat.
All at the ready
because
you never know
it keeps changing.

In summer
I'd even get over my fear of rope swings
dive in
knees tucked
screaming unafraid.
then watch the approaching storm with you
both of us waiting for the first shout from the sky.

Anticipating,
not unlike the way I felt sitting next to you
on the second day I knew you.

It Starts At Home

At 8:15 in the morning
everyone
myself
look into their bathroom mirrors.

Opaque with steam
speckled with blue toothpaste.

Fleshy bags under bloodshot eyes
we think to ourselves
"I look like hell."

In Yakima
Steve
shaves his head in long strokes
back to front
blinks in the dim light
"what next?"

In Florida
Angela
brushes her hair
and decides to pull it back into a ponytail.

Decisions are made
large
small.

Someone else considers
overthrowing the government,
or buying a bagel on the way to work,
or eating a kiwi in the car,
tossing limp brown rinds out the window.

In all these mirrors
personal
political
revolution begins at home
especially in the bathroom mirror.

The Inner Trump

Embrace your inner Trump
indulge him a little
he is in all of us.

Find the lie
tell it brazenly
it'll be easier to be honest after that.

Let him think he's in charge:
to be good all the time
is impossible.
Acknowledge it
move on.

You were in a hurry
you ran a red light.
You were selfish
you were drunk
you were horny
you were hungry.

This is normal.
It will be easier to be kind
once you forgive yourself
for unkindness.

Yes, kindness is important
we should do a kindness
as often as possible
But when you don't
shake it off
let it go.

Embrace the Trump in you
but let him know
it isn't going to happen every day.
He'll sulk
call you a loser

he's just acting out.

See, your inner Trump
is not running the country
there will be no nuclear war
if you indulge him.

Your inner Trump
would have to be very small
to fit inside you.

You can take him
you have the power.

Embrace him.

Silence him.

Truth And Order

The man who shouts "Jesus Christ"
when a nurse tries to help him out of his chair
wants to be left alone.

I wonder why
she doesn't leave him there.

Mom is in a wheelchair.
I push her from the music room
to the sun room.
A Lawrence Welk DVD is playing.
My mom and I talk about nothing over it.

Her nails are painted red
Her hair neatly done up
as if she'd been to the stylist this morning.
She has on yellow pants
and a light green shirt with flower prints.

Again.
She thinks I am her brother
introduces me as such
when the nurse brings her meds.

My obsessive need for truth
has me shaking my head no to the nurse
as if she needed to be told that.

There is some order but very little truth.

In the material world
in the changing of the seasons
in the blades of grass that all look the same
there is order there.

And I do take comfort in that
but wonder if it will change someday.

With my Mom there is some truth
in what she says
but very little order.
It's good for me, I think.

The cycle of life
I guess there is some order there.
We are born
we are completely dependent
if we are lucky
we learn survival skills.
Then we grow old
completely dependent on others.
It's almost funny
a sick joke played on everyone.

For years I raged against the sappy and sentimental
now I'm here watching a Lawrence Welk special.

There are moments
when my Mom looks over at me with
what I imagine is a
Can you believe this shit expression.
This is during the orchestra's
take on
Take the A Train
that doesn't rock
or roll
let alone swing.

So I talk to her about dancing at a wedding
with a woman I barely knew
attempting to dip her
dropping her.
She laughed.

So does Mom.
Even though
she doesn't understand the story
a fall is still funny.

The marriage we were celebrating
lasted less than a year.
I do not tell Mom that part.

I mean what do I expect?
A screening of *The Decline of Western Civilization?*
Sid and Nancy?
for the old folks?
If I feel there is more truth in there
than any goddamn Lawrence Welk special
it's my truth
not theirs.

My Mom's truths are hard to see,
or tell.
When she mentions going home I answer.
"Someday Mom, someday."

Wishes And Plantains

I wish it would rain again
The other day I walked in it
wasn't half bad.

I wish the sun would come out
I would sit outside
till the warmth
made me sleepy
in the light.

I wish for a lot of things right now
hardly any attainable
so I get up
do what I have to
eat a meal
clean up after
slice up soft
spotted
black-skinned plantains
fry them in grapeseed oil
salt
watch closely
turn them with tongs
divvy them up
between two small plates
give one to my Dad.

He compliments me on them.
We agree we do not like them
yellow
green or firm.
We agree on
the best time to fry plantains
we agree on their sweetness.
I eat too quickly
spear one after another
with a small fork
why am I rushing?

What I am I rushing to?
Would I enjoy them more
if I slowed down?

Sushi slows me down
chopsticks slow me down
wasabi burning
the top of my tongue
back of my throat.
A small bowl of soy sauce
a little green heat added.
The sushi rolls go there first
then to my plate
I am not methodical about much
I'm chaos personified
sushi slows me down.
Dad folds a piece of pickled ginger
places it atop each roll
I laugh a little
at him
near him
with him.

Outside

Outside
rain so light
it hardly qualifies
as precipitation.

Birds are out
manic mockingbirds
get me wondering
about evolution
and how they got to be
call collectors.

Robins hop
across wet grass
cock their heads
one way
the other
listening for worms.

I remember the robin
last year
who would stand
under our suet cage
fly up
hover
peck out
a morsel of fat
then back down
to terra firma.

In nature
the robin
does not know
it's a robin.
No one ever said
"You are a robin
When you're not flying
you hug the earth."

DNA
instinct
whatever.
That robin
maybe tired of worms
broke the chain.

Maybe
I was tired
of sitting at home
and forced myself
to don a maroon ball-cap
bright orange slicker
and take a walk.
I broke the chain
inertia
boredom
malaise
dread.

The birds were out
even one
I couldn't identify
that was probably
a woodpecker of some sort.

In Which I Try To Connect Ghosts
Fitted Sheets
and Yoga Class

"I don't believe in ghosts"
I told a friend.
Then,
as if to contradict myself
I told her that I saw
my dead grandmother
in the doorway to my bedroom
late at night.
She made no attempt to communicate
just stood there sternly
staring
at her seven-year-old grandson.

My late mother comes to mind
when I try to fold a fitted sheet.
I once told her
I was never going to learn how.
She told me
I was too negative.

She stands beside me
shaking her head
as if it is her failure.
I tell her
that I got all the important stuff
kindness
empathy
from her.
Turns out that's what
she needs to hear.
She has learned that
folding fitted sheets
ain't shit.

My dead grandmother

in that doorway
was a dream.

Our family shifts
alters
grows.
We all get together
and I hold my newest grandniece.
I go downstairs
and play synthesizer
and guitar
with her older sister.
It's just noise
lovely chaos.
The more I remind myself
that order is not natural
the happier I am.

My late mother
would look down
and laugh
if she could—
but she can't
because heaven doesn't exist.
Or it does
but it's here on earth.

I think about her every day.
That is heaven.
We laugh about the time
she was upset
because the meat pie was cold
and she laughs too
because death
means letting go of everything.

In yoga class
I try to get out of my head.
Sometimes all the doors are locked
and I wander the bright walls

of my brain.

My balance is off
but so is everyone else
we are all but slim trees
in a stiff breeze.
I'm ten minutes from home
in a warrior position.
It's as close as I come to prayer.

Contradiction

There are no revelations
only slow, hard work
tiny victories
my eyes sting from the smoke
of far off or
nearby battles.

What there is
is the sweat drying on your forehead
a heart-shaped smile
crab cakes with red pepper sauce
and other revelations.

Perfect Peach

I want to write about it
stubbled
round
drops of water clinging to it
a single cleft
running down the side
from the top.

First bite
presents a pale orange
doorway
juice runs down my chin.

My late mother
had no passion for food.
I would think that even she
would appreciate it
the woman who
when she heard a news story
that full meals would be replaced
by a pill
said "what a great idea!"

Even she
would eat the peach
laugh a little
stress a little
about the juice
running down her chin
reach for a napkin.

I'd like to think
she'd eat around the pit
tear off the last hanging piece
of sweet ragged flesh
sidearm that pit into the brush.
Like I did this morning
but not before

a small prayer
thanking whomever
for the perfect peach.

Dark Hours

Hold them in your hand
they pulse
instead of tick
they beat and they are alive
put them back where you got them
keep them warm
with a scarf or blanket.

Heavy with dark
The hours are heavy with dark
dark that I could push my hand in.
Squeeze the dark hours dry
drink the black juices
that run between my fingers.
Lick residual drops
off the palms of my hands
drink down the dark night's black juices.

Picking My Grandmother Up

I was still half asleep
when I helped you up.
Behind you,
a trail of flattened shag rug
showed me how you'd dragged yourself
from the kitchen.

When the pain made you scream
I was awake after that.
I made the appropriate phone calls
ambulance
my dad
not really thinking about any of it.

You would light your cigarettes off the stove
wearing that lime green bathrobe
that would hang loosely,
the sleeve dropping dangerously close
to the glowing orange coil of the burner.

And then, forgetting we had ash trays
you would bring
crooked, lip-sticked butt ends outside
to put them out.
And that was what you were doing
when you fell.

Hank Williams In My Kitchen

The cassette is terrible.
the right songs are on it
but they're loaded down
with awful syrupy string arrangements
that my father insists aren't on the originals.

So when Hank appears in my kitchen
I assume that he wants to protest,
to stand there
say "no goddamned way."
But he just looks depressed.

I offer him a seat
apologize for not having any strong stuff.
Herbal tea won't cut it.
He produces two small white pills
places them on the table
takes his hat off
places it next to the pills
stares at all of it.

His hair is sparse
skin stretched tight
across his lean face.

I get him a glass of water
to wash the pills down.
He mutters thanks
doesn't look at me.
In an instant
the pills are gone.

I don't know what else to do.
I wish it were just me and that
lousy goddamned tape again.

Night Shift

Working nights
in a security guard shack
at a power plant.
I'd go crazy from boredom
huddle obsessively over the radio
twisting the tuner back and forth
trying to find decent rock n' roll.

Every hour I'd get in my car
make my rounds.

Another guard
in another shack
at the opposite end of the plant.

His name was Bill
he'd get juiced
call me
three in the morning
tell me about Vietnam,
how he was in the bush country
and his latest sexual conquest.

He was fired when supervisors
found a pile
of beer cans outside his shack.

A co-worker told me
Bill was crazy
all short fuses and booze
but that one time we talked
he never lost it with me.
No, he opened up
told me damned near everything about himself.

Of course that could have just been the beer talking
maybe there was no real trust
just a need to talk to someone
90

anyone
at three in the morning
on the coldest goddamn night of the year.

The Frozen Painter

One summer the house-painter froze in mid-stroke. The people who hired him were already annoyed that he was working too slowly. Now it seemed for certain that he would never finish. They had the idea of moving him, frozen paint-brush and all, to the front yard and to charge money to see him. It was unique; a man going about his day, suddenly freezing solid. And he inspired people to quit their jobs and do what they really wanted to do. The mailman left his job and wrote a novel. The garbageman stopped collecting trash and devoted all his time to his band. The gardener began to sculpt again. And the piano teacher decided to help the poor instead. And they were all secretly grateful to the frozen painter. Who looked beautiful in falling snow, trussed in holiday lights, the curled frozen paintbrush extended upward and ahead of him like a torch.

At The Rainbow Cafe Teen Canteen
In Chamberlain, South Dakota 1957

All around you
they dance their own steps
while you dance yours
in the middle of the room
an island
among all the other jitterbugging kids.

T-shirt
black shoes
dangerous crewcut
a half-crouch
head cocked
arms out.

The others are scared
the pleasure you take in solitude
you don't care.

You are in a club in South Dakota
the music is on
guitar
drums
the hiccup of the rockabilly vocal
nothing else matters.

Roux

In my dreams I make roux
dark, thick
the color of peanut butter
and I toss in
celery, pepper, onions
cook over a medium heat
wine, tomato paste, and broth
all go in later.

I am careful with my roux
it starts on a low heat
flour and oil
flour and butter
barely enough to cover
the bottom of the pan
I drag a wooden spoon in slow circles
creating a path that closes
as quickly as it opens.

Someday I will make
a stew
etouffée
something that needs a roux
for someone I love
it will demonstrate my patience
she might even watch it with me
together we will stare down
into the pot
as if it held the answer
to every important question
we ever had.

Don Fisher has been writing
poetry, fiction and non-fiction
for 40 plus years. This is his
first book. He lives and writes
in Chicopee, Massachusetts
where he gets through the
pandemic with poetry, punk
rock, hip hop, old-school
country and by taking turns
cooking elaborate meals with
his father. He should take
more walks.

www.ingramcontent.com/pod-product-compliance
Lightning Source LLC
Chambersburg PA
CBHW071158090426
42736CB00012B/2374